SUGAR PIE
LULLABY

THE SOUL
OF MOTOWN
IN A SONG
OF LOVE

sourcebooks
eXplore

CAROLE BOSTON
WEATHERFORD

PICTURES BY
SAWYER CLOUD

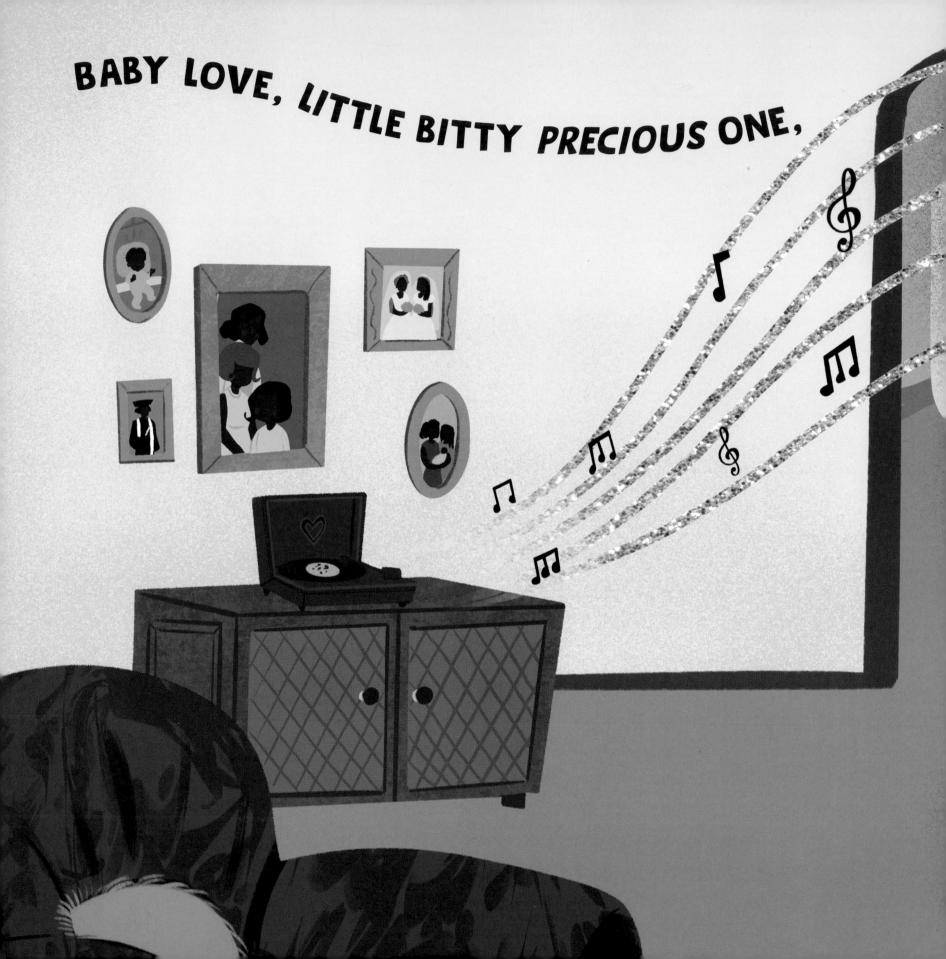

WHAT ELSE IS THERE TO DO?

MORNING, NOON, AND NIGHT
ALL I DO *IS* THANK GOD FOR YOU.

SHOO-BEE-DO-BEE-DO-BEE-DO-DAH-DAY!
I'M YOUR PUPPET.
YOU REALLY GOT A HOLD ON ME.

I CAN'T HELP MYSELF.
DO I DO, GOTTA HAVE YOU.

THE WAY YOU DO THE THINGS YOU DO,
YOU'RE MY DREAM COME TRUE.
SWEETNESS, YOU'RE MY EVERYTHING.

IF I WERE A CARPENTER,
IF THIS WORLD WERE MINE,
I COULD BUILD MY WHOLE WORLD AROUND YOU.
GOD BLESS WHOEVER SENT YOU.

BABY, BABY DON'T CRY.
YOU'RE ALL I NEED TO GET BY.
YOUR DREAMS TAKE WINGS AND FLY.

DON'T YOU WORRY
          'BOUT A THING.
REACH OUT, I'LL BE THERE.

OOO, BABY BABY,
  WITH EACH BEAT OF MY HEART,
  OH HOW HAPPY, OH HOW HAPPY.

MY DAILY PRAYER, YOU WILL KNOW
WHERE PEACEFUL WATERS FLOW.
YOU'VE MADE ME SO VERY HAPPY.

SIGNED, SEALED,
DELIVERED, I'M YOURS.

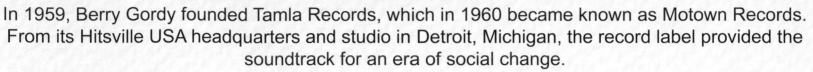

AUTHOR'S NOTE

In 1959, Berry Gordy founded Tamla Records, which in 1960 became known as Motown Records. From its Hitsville USA headquarters and studio in Detroit, Michigan, the record label provided the soundtrack for an era of social change.

As a child of the 1960s, I grew up on the Motown sound. The first records that I ever bought were 45s by The Supremes. With my neighborhood friends, Robin and Christine, I sang the Supremes' hits under red spotlights in the basement. We were something else! Following are just a few of my favorite songs from this historic era with a little extra information for you to enjoy.

"I CAN'T HELP MYSELF (SUGAR PIE, HONEY BUNCH)"
Written by Brian Holland, Lamont Dozier, and Eddie Holland
Recorded by the Four Tops in 1965 for Motown Records

The Four Tops' career-making single remained popular throughout the sixties and seventies—and even today.

"BABY LOVE"
Written by Brian Holland, Lamont Dozier, and Eddie Holland
Recorded by the Supremes in 1964 for Motown Records

One of the Supremes' fourteen U.S. top ten hits, this song was—according to Dozier—about his first love, who inspired several Motown songs.

"LITTLE BITTY PRETTY ONE"
Written by Bobby Day
Recorded by Bobby Day
and the Satellites in 1957 for Class

This catchy dance tune was covered by another singer, Thurston Harris, whose version soared to number two on the R&B chart and made it to number six on the U.S. Billboard Best-Sellers chart.

"BORN TO LOVE YOU"
Written by Ivy Jo Hunter and William "Mickey" Stevenson
Recorded by the Temptations in 1965 for Gordy Records

This song is from *The Temptin' Temptations*, the third, and some say the best, album by the Temptations.

"WHAT ELSE IS THERE TO DO (BUT THINK ABOUT YOU)"
Written by Stevie Wonder, Clarence Paul, and Morris Broadnax
Recorded by the Four Tops in 1967 for Motown Records

This song is from the album *Reach Out*, which featured six singles that charted in the top twenty and was the group's last to be produced by Motown's main songwriting team.

"YOU ARE THE SUNSHINE OF MY LIFE"
Written by Stevie Wonder
Recorded by Stevie Wonder in 1973 for Motown Records

A heartfelt expression of true love, this song is one of Wonder's thirty top ten hits. A true musical genius, he has sold more than one hundred million records and won twenty-two Grammy Awards.

"MORNING, NOON AND NIGHT"
Written by Charles Calhoun
Recorded by Big Joe Turner in 1958 for Atlantic Records

American blues singer-songwriter Doc Pomus once said that rock and roll would have never happened without Joe Turner, who gained fame in the 1950s from recordings like this song. Turner was inducted into the Rock & Roll Hall of Fame in 1987.

"ALL I DO IS THINK ABOUT YOU"
Written by Stevie Wonder,
Clarence Paul, and Morris Broadnax
Recorded by Tammi Terrell in 1966 for Motown Records

With a cool beat and stunning vocals, this hit song made Tammi Terrell one of Motown's brightest stars of the 1960s.

"SHOO-BE-DOO-BE-DOO-DA-DAY"
Written by Stevie Wonder, Sylvia Moy,
and Henry Cosby
Recorded by Stevie Wonder in 1968 for Motown Records

Released as a single, this was the first to showcase Wonder's talent at the clavinet. It reached number nine on the Billboard Hot 100 pop singles chart in 1968 and was number one on the R&B chart.

"I'M YOUR PUPPET"
Written by Dan Penn and Spooner Oldham
Recorded by James & Bobby Purify
in 1966 for Bell Records

This single from the album *James & Bobby Purify* was nominated for a Grammy Award for Best R&B Performance by a Duo or Group with Vocals in 1967.

"YOU'VE REALLY GOT A HOLD ON ME"
Written by Smokey Robinson
Recorded by the Miracles in 1962 for Tamla Records

Tamla Records was the first of various Motown labels founded by Berry Gordy Jr. Formed in 1959, Tamla Records was home to such Motown legends as Smokey Robinson, Marvin Gaye, Stevie Wonder, and the Marvelettes. Tamla Records remained in operation until 1986.

"DO I DO"
Written by Stevie Wonder
Recorded by Stevie Wonder
in 1982 for Tamla Records

This song hit number thirteen on the Billboard Hot 100 chart in the U.S. The album version of the song is ten minutes long and features a rare example of Wonder rapping near the end. Jazz icon Dizzy Gillespie also provides a trumpet solo near the end.

"GOTTA HAVE YOU"
Written by Stevie Wonder
Recorded by Stevie Wonder
in 1991 for Motown Records

This song was the first release from the 1991 soundtrack to the film *Jungle Fever*. It peaked at number the in the Hot R&B/Hip-Hop Songs chart. It was one of Wonder's few top ten songs of the nineties.

"THE WAY YOU DO THE THINGS YOU DO"
Written by Smokey Robinson
and Bobby Rogers
Recorded by the Temptations
in 1964 for Motown Records

This hit song was the Temptations' first charting single on the Billboard Hot 100, peaking at number eleven. When the Temptations heard the news, they shed tears of joy!

"(YOU'RE MY) DREAM COME TRUE"
Written by Berry Gordy Jr.
Recorded by the Temptations in 1962 for Gordy Records

This song was the first-ever release on the brand-new Gordy Records imprint of Motown and was the first chart hit. It was also Eddie Kendricks's first lead vocal on a Temptations record.

"YOU'RE MY EVERYTHING"
Written by Rodger Penzabene,
Cornelius Grant, and Norman Whitfield
Recorded by the Temptations
in 1967 for Motown Records

This single, the first of four songs co-written by Rodger Penzabene, reached number three on the U.S. Billboard R&B chart and number six on the U.S. Billboard pop chart.

"IF I WERE A CARPENTER"
Written by Tim Hardin
Recorded by Tim Hardin in 1967 for Motown Records

Folk singer Tim Hardin performed this song at Woodstock, a famously huge outdoor music festival. It is about a man asking an elegant woman if she would still love and marry him if he were just a carpenter.

"IF THIS WORLD WERE MINE"
Written by Marvin Gaye
Recorded by Marvin Gaye
and Tammi Terrell in 1970 for Motown Records

First released as a single in 1967, this song reached number sixty-eight on the Billboard Hot 100 chart and twenty-seven on the Billboard Hot R&B singles chart. During his last tours in the 1980s, Gaye performed this song, as well as other hits that he had recorded with Terrell.

"IF I COULD BUILD MY WHOLE WORLD AROUND YOU"
Written by Harvey Fuqua, Johnny Bristol,
and Vernon Bullock
Recorded by Marvin Gaye and Tammi Terrell
in 1967 for Motown Records

This popular song was Gaye and Terrell's third duet and was one of the few songs for the duo not written by hitmakers Ashford and Simpson.

"GOD BLESS WHOEVER SENT YOU"
Written by Clay McMurray and Pam Sawyer
Recorded by the Originals in 1970 for Motown Records

This gospel-infused love song opens with the sound of bells, followed by a slow cymbal roll and eventually the group's sweet, soft vocals.

"BABY BABY DON'T CRY"
Written by Smokey Robinson,
Al Cleveland, and Terry Johnson
Recorded by the Miracles in 1968 for Motown Records

Noted for Robinson's spoken words at the beginning and before the second verse, this song is a testament to heartbreak.

"YOU'RE ALL I NEED TO GET BY"
Written by Nickolas Ashford and Valerie Simpson
Recorded by Marvin Gaye and Tammi Terrell
in 1968 for Tamla Records

One of the last recordings by Gaye and Terrell, this touching song incorporates vocals from a New York church choir.

"WHEN YOUR DREAMS TAKE WINGS AND FLY"
Written by Bruce Gray, Leroy Green, and Norman Harris
Recorded by the Four Tops in 1978 for ABC Records

This song from the Four Tops' last album for ABC will get you dancing for sure!

"DON'T YOU WORRY 'BOUT A THING"
Written by Stevie Wonder
Recorded by Stevie Wonder in 1973 for Motown Records

On this Latin soul hit, Wonder encourages his love to explore life fearlessly, knowing that he will always be by her side. Despite the Latin lyrics, Wonder doesn't even speak Spanish.

"REACH OUT I'LL BE THERE"
Written by Brian Holland,
Lamont Dozier, and Eddie Holland
Recorded by the Four Tops
in 1966 for Motown Records

The Four Tops recorded this in just two takes and didn't have big expectations for it. Motown boss Berry Gordy Jr., however, had a knack for identifying hits and released it as a single. It went on to be number one for weeks and is one of Motown's best-known tunes of the sixties!

"OOO BABY BABY"
Written by Smokey Robinson and Warren "Pete" Moore
Recorded by the Miracles in 1965 for Motown Records

This classic Motown hit has been so popular over the years that it has been covered by many artists, from Ella Fitzgerald to Lenny Kravitz.

"WITH EACH BEAT OF MY HEART"

Written by Stevie Wonder
Recorded by Stevie Wonder
in 1987 for Motown Records

Released quickly and beloved by listeners, the album including this fan favorite topped the R&B charts for seven weeks!

"OH HOW HAPPY"
Written by Edwin Starr
Recorded by the Shades of Blue
in 1966 for Impact Records

This record's release took the group by surprise. Out one night with friends, they happened to hear their song on the radio. People loved it, and it soared to the top of the charts.

"MY DAILY PRAYER"
Written by Amos Milburn and Clarence Paul
Recorded by Amos Milburn in 1963 for Motown Records

In this song, Milburn's energetic voice shows his star power. It's impossible not to smile when he slips his own name into the lyrics.

"YOU WILL KNOW"
Written by Stevie Wonder
Recorded by Stevie Wonder
in 1987 for Motown Records

This second single from the album *Characters* hit number seventy-seven on the Billboard Hot 100, topped Billboard's Hot R&B Songs chart for a week in March of 1988, and peaked at number sixteen on Billboard's Adult Contemporary chart.

"WHERE PEACEFUL WATERS FLOW"
Written by Jim Weatherly
Recorded by Jim Weatherly in 1973 for RCA Records

Jim Weatherly began writing songs as a teenager, forming his own bands while in high school and at the University of Mississippi, which he attended on a football scholarship. Although a star quarterback at Ole Miss, he chose a career in music over football and went on to write songs for almost fifty years.

"YOU'VE MADE ME SO VERY HAPPY"
Written by Brenda Holloway, Patrice Holloway, Frank Wilson, and Berry Gordy Jr.
Recorded by Brenda Holloway in 1967 for Tamla Records

Singer-songwriter Brenda Holloway felt that no matter what, she wanted to always know her strength and remember the beauty in life. This hit single reflects her upbeat outlook.

"MERCY MERCY ME"
Written by Marvin Gaye
Recorded by Marvin Gaye
in 1971 for Tamla Records

This song reflects the environmental destruction that was in the news at the time. Berry Gordy Jr. feared that a song about environmentalism wouldn't sell, but was proven wrong when this song rose to the number one R&B song and to number four on the Billboard Hot 100.

"HEAVEN MUST HAVE SENT YOU"
Written by Brian Holland, Lamont Dozier, and Eddie Holland
Recorded by the Elgins
in 1966 for Motown Records

This song may have secured the Elgins' place in the history of soul music. It reached number nine on the Billboard Hot R&B chart, and number fifty on the Billboard Hot 100.

"SIGNED, SEALED, DELIVERED (I'M YOURS)"
Written by Stevie Wonder, Syreeta, Lee Garrett, and Lula Mae Hardaway
Recorded by Stevie Wonder in 1970 for Motown Records

This song was the first single Wonder produced on his own and was also the first to feature his female backup singing group, composed of Lynda Laurence (who went on to become a member of the Supremes), Syreeta Wright (who also cowrote the song), and Venetta Fields. In 2008, he credited the song title and chorus to his mother, Lula Mae.

POET AND AUTHOR CAROLE BOSTON WEATHERFORD has written more than sixty books that have won numerous awards, including the Newbery Honor, Coretta Scott King Author Award and Honor, two NAACP Image Awards, two Caldecott Medals, a WNDB Walter Award, and a Robert F. Sibert Honor. She often writes about African American history, families and traditions, and jazz.

SAWYER CLOUD is a freelance artist living in Madagascar, her native country. Her passion for kids' literature pushed her to turn illustrating into a living as she just couldn't consider any other occupation than creating pictures for children. After working on many independent projects, she managed to build a career as an illustrator, got represented by a reputable agency in 2020, and worked on many titles with most of the major publishers in kids publishing. Sawyer loves sunny days and music, and dreams of owning a small cottage and traveling the world. She lives with her family and her two pets, Arya the dog and Potter the cat.

Text © 2023 by Carole Boston Weatherford • Illustrations © 2023 by Sawyer Cloud • Cover and internal design © 2023 by Sourcebooks
Sourcebooks and the colophon are registered trademarks of Sourcebooks. • All rights reserved. • The characters and events portrayed in this
book are fictitious or are used fictitiously. Any similarity to real persons, living or dead, is purely coincidental and not intended by the author.
The illustrations of the book were created on iPad Pro with Procreate. • Published by Sourcebooks eXplore, an imprint of Sourcebooks Kids
P.O. Box 4410, Naperville, Illinois 60567-4410 • (630) 961-3900 • sourcebookskids.com • Cataloging-in-Publication Data is on file with the
Library of Congress. • Source of Production: 1010 Printing Asia Limited, Kwun Tong, Hong Kong, China • Date of Production: August 2022
Run Number: 5026959 • Printed and bound in China. • OGP 10 9 8 7 6 5 4 3 2 1

The Girl Who Wanted to Hunt

A SIBERIAN TALE

retold
by
Emery
Bernhard

pictures
by
Durga
Bernhard

HOLIDAY HOUSE • NEW YORK

Jacket and book design by Durga Bernhard

Library of Congress Cataloging-in-Publication Data
Bernhard, Emery.
The girl who wanted to hunt : a Siberian tale / retold by Emery
Bernhard ; illustrated by Durga Bernhard. — 1st ed.
p.   cm.
Summary: A young girl uses her skills as a hunter to avenge her
father's death and to escape her evil stepmother.
ISBN 0-8234-1125-7
[1. Folklore—Russia (Federation)—Siberia.]   I. Bernhard, Durga,
ill.   II. Title.
PZ8.1.B4165Gi   1994   93-48024   CIP   AC
398.21—dc20
[E]

For our
brave and beautiful
daughter Eve,
and for the
living memory of
her great-grandmother,
Regina Loewy Werner,
who would have
loved her.

ittle Anga was a child of the *taiga*, the endless forest of Siberia. She lived in a hut by the Amur River with her mother and father. Her mother cooked food and wove baskets, softened animal skins and embroidered robes. Her father hunted deer, elk, bear, sable, and boar—and he talked to all the wild creatures, even the great tiger.

"Thank you for giving us food to eat," said Adiga, Anga's father, whenever he hunted. And since Adiga's spears and arrows always hit their target, little Anga was never hungry.

Then the Black Death came to the people living along the Amur. It carried away Anga's mother, and Anga was left alone with her father.

Adiga loved his little girl very much, but he was also scared for her. Who would take care of her while he was hunting? Who would show her how to cook food and weave baskets, how to soften animal skins and embroider robes?

Adiga brought home a new wife. Her name was Unin, and she was lazy. She spent her days eating and sleeping and drinking tea by the fire.

"Husband," declared Unin, "you must make toys to get Anga used to the chores she will do for me."

So Adiga made Anga a small bowl and a tiny cradle, a leather scraper, and a little sewing needle.

Anga thanked Adiga, yet she did not touch the toys.

"These are nice, Father, but I want to play with hunting toys. When I grow up I will be a hunter like you."

Unin scowled. "Hunting is not a girl's work!" she insisted.

But Adiga saw in Anga's eyes that she spoke the truth.

Adiga made Anga a spear and a small bow and arrows. He carved little wooden hunting dogs and a wooden reindeer. And he began teaching Anga how to talk to all the wild creatures, even the great tiger.

Unin was furious. She teased Anga about her new toys and taunted Adiga whenever he returned from hunting.

"A skinny deer, a few raccoons, a squirrel—how can you teach your daughter to hunt when this is all you bring home to your hungry wife? Can't you kill something bigger, a nice fat bear or a boar at least?"

One day, Adiga tracked a wild boar into the *taiga*. With Unin's words ringing in his ears, he moved quickly, eager to spear the big animal. Suddenly, there was squealing and roaring in the bushes. A tiger had seen the boar!

Adiga raised his spear. The tiger and the boar were scuffling and thrashing and kicking up dust and leaves, and Adiga could not tell one animal from the other.

"Go away, tiger!" he yelled. "This boar is for me!" Adiga hurled his spear blindly into the bush. The spear grazed the tiger. Now the wounded beast hissed with rage.

"How dare you harm me just to get food!" snarled the tiger. "No one steals from me and lives to tell of it! I will be the last thing you ever see!"

The tiger charged at Adiga and killed him.

Anga had no time to mourn her father's death. From sunrise to sunset she was busy doing chores for her stepmother—who spent her own days sleeping and eating and telling Anga what to do.

"Girl, I'm cold," complained Unin. "Gather more firewood. And how can you expect me to keep warm in my old worn-out robe? Make me a new robe with reindeer hair! I'll give you no food until my new robe is ready."

Anga knew she should do as she was told, but the reindeer were gone for the summer. How could she get reindeer fur for a new robe? She was lonely and hungry, and she missed her father. Anga found the wooden animals Adiga had made and brought them outside.

"Is your belly empty, too?" she asked, putting her toy reindeer down in a patch of grass. "Go ahead and eat."

With a snort, the reindeer suddenly came to life! He stamped his hooves and bobbed his head. "Thank you," he said, munching some green leaves. "Now, dear Anga, I will help you."

The reindeer grew and grew, his shaggy hair growing longer and longer. When he was as tall as Anga, he shook off all his hair. Then the reindeer shrank back into a wooden toy.

Anga gathered the hair and sewed it into a robe for Unin.

"So you've tricked me!" said Unin, grabbing the robe. "You didn't do this yourself! Now I am hungry. Bring me something to eat. Go fill my baskets with fish by nightfall, or no food for you!"

Anga knew it would take many days to fill the baskets with fish. Taking the spear her father had given her, she made her way along the bank of the river until she came to a shallow pool. A huge fish was thrashing in the water. Anga raised her spear and aimed.

"Wait!" wheezed the big fish, "I'm stranded! Help me back into the deep water, and I'll bring you all the fish you need!"

Anga waded into the pool and pushed the fish into the river. No sooner had it dived into the current than it reappeared by the riverbank, waiting for Anga to take dozens of little fish out of its mouth. She filled the baskets with fish and carried them home to her stepmother.

Unin soon grew tired of eating fish. "You say you want to hunt. Well go ahead, bring me something with real fat on it."

Anga took her spear and entered the *taiga*. She stepped carefully and stopped often to listen. She stalked up and down hills and across streams until she came to a bright grove of birch trees. Sitting down with her back against a tree, Anga closed her eyes and rested. The trunk gently rocked her as it swayed in the wind. After a few minutes, Anga thanked the birch tree, and was about to leave when a hoarse growl came from the bushes.

A tiger slowly padded towards her with his head low and his eyes gleaming. "Who are you and why are you here?" demanded the tiger.

"I am Anga, daughter of Adiga," said the bold girl, grabbing her spear. "Are you the tiger who killed my father?"

"What if I am?" sneered the tiger. "You're just a little girl. I'll eat you the same way I ate your father!"

"Go away, evil one!" shouted Anga, quickly climbing the birch tree. The tiger roared and leaped at the girl, tearing off one of her boots. Anga felt the beast's hot breath on her bare foot.

Suddenly, she heard the voice of the tree. "Be brave, dear Anga, for I will help you."

The tree began to tremble and shake. Scrambling and clawing at the slippery bark, the tiger slid down into a fork in the trunk. The thick branches squeezed around the tiger so tightly that he could not escape. He squirmed and cowered as Anga jumped to the ground and aimed her spear.

"You killed my father! Any tiger who becomes a man-eater must be put to death. I will be the last thing you ever see!"

She flung her spear at the tiger.

People up and down the Amur River began telling the tale of the brave girl who killed a raging tiger. Unin's belly was full of the meat Anga brought home, but she shared none of it with her stepdaughter. Nothing Anga did could please her.

"You got lucky with your hunting, but your cooking tastes like mud. And this robe you made is so ugly that I can't wear it. You're as useless as my sick old grandmother. Go find me some ginseng root. I need ginseng tea to make me strong."

Anga drifted into the *taiga*, picking berries and searching for ginseng. The wind whispered through the trees, carrying a sound like faraway weeping. Anga moved toward the sound. Crouching in the pine needles was an old woman wrapped in a fishskin robe, singing quietly to herself. It was Unin's grandmother.

"What's the matter, Grandmother? Are you sick?" Anga asked.

"A little tired, perhaps," replied the old woman. "I've been looking for my cane. I can't walk far without it."

Anga gave the old woman a piece of ginseng root to chew and found a sturdy branch she could use as a walking stick.

"Is there anything else I can do for you, Grandmother?"

"No, dear Anga," said the elder. "I feel stronger already. You have shown me kindness, and now I'll help you with this warning. Do not go to sleep tonight, for my granddaughter Unin means to kill you! You must be brave, my child."

Anga was late returning home. "Where is my ginseng?" demanded Unin. "And where is my firewood for the night?"

Anga gave the root to Unin, did her chores, and went to bed. But she did not go to sleep. Soon she heard her stepmother moving about in the darkness. The fire in the hearth began burning brightly as Unin started throwing things into the flames.

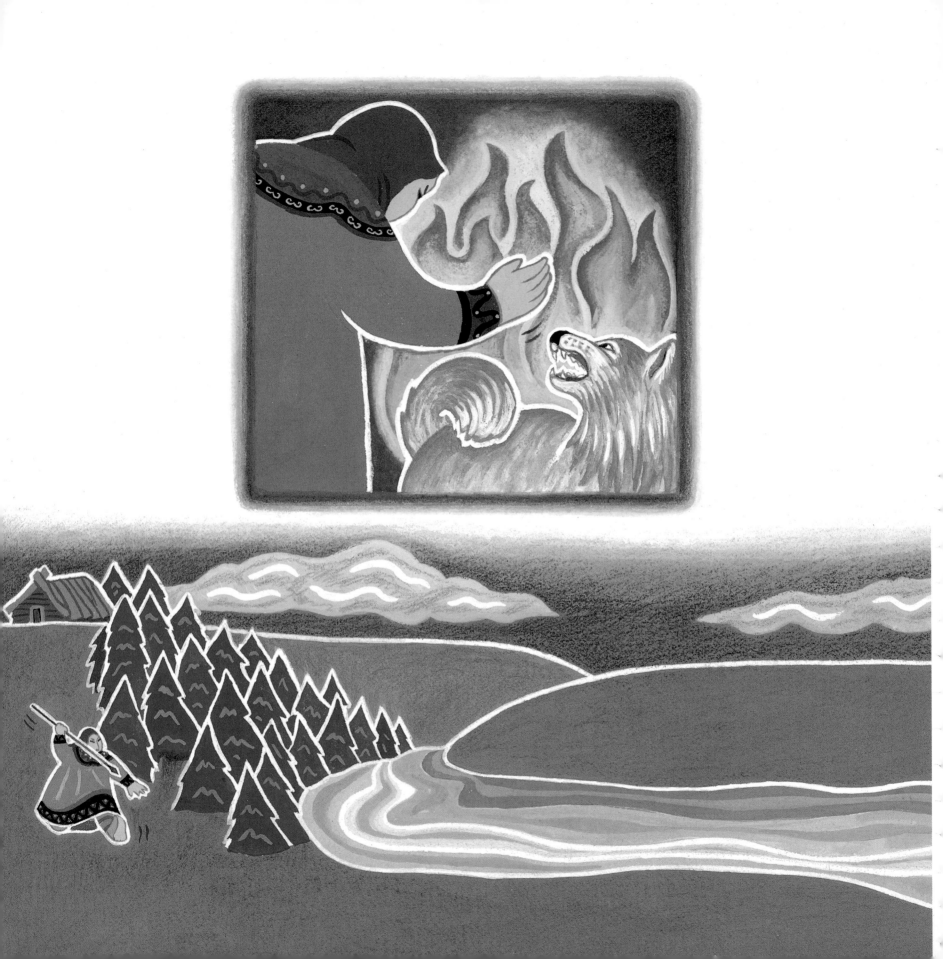

Into the fire went Anga's small bow, her arrows, and her toy reindeer. Unin began to throw in the wooden hunting dogs, one by one. As she picked up the last of the toy dogs, it came alive and snapped at Unin! Barking and whining, it jumped to the ground and bounded over to the girl.

"Be quick, dear Anga. We must run! I'll show you the way!"

Anga and her dog ran down to the river. The Moon was rising. A moonbeam stretched a ribbon of light across the water, and Anga followed the dog along the moonbeam path.

Unin grabbed Anga's spear and lurched after them, cursing and shaking her fist. When she hauled herself onto the ribbon of light, the shimmering moonbeam broke under her weight. Unin fell into the cold water with a great splash.

Unin stood and hurled the spear at Anga. The spear flew up to the girl and stopped, saying, "Do not fear, dear Anga, for I will never harm you. Someday you will hunt with me again." Then the spear turned, diving back toward Unin.

Unin's eyes grew wide, bulging with terror as the spear plunged closer and closer. Just as it was about to strike, Unin's arms became wings and her feet grew claws. She turned into a big-eyed owl and flew off to the *taiga*, hooting her name over and over, "OOOO-nin . . . OOOO-nin . . ."

Anga's spear fell into the Amur River and was never seen again.

Anga and her dog ran along the moonbeam path all the way to the Moon.

"Welcome to your new home, dear Anga," said the Moon, hugging the girl with long, pale arms. "You will always be safe here."

The moonbeam path disappeared as the Sun came up.

Every night, Anga waits for the Moon to rise. Then she runs along the moonbeam path that stretches down to Earth. She searches everywhere for her lost spear, for she will not hunt without it. She shines her soft light in the eyes of sleeping children. And if she sees tears in a child's eyes, she kisses them away and whispers, "Don't worry, dear child. I will help you. Here is a sweet dream."

But if Anga hears the owl cry, "OOO-nin . . . OOO-nin . . . ," she hurries back up the moonbeam path.

It is said that people can see Anga and her dog at night when the Moon is up and the sky is clear. You can see her too, if you open your eyes when the Moon shines its soft silvery light on you.

Author's Note

The Girl Who Wanted to Hunt is a variation on the ancient theme of the evil stepmother. From *Vasalisa the Wise* to *Cinderella*, we find tales throughout the world of innocent and ill-used stepdaughters who must leave home to survive, or who in the end must confront or come to terms with a beast or witch. Versions of *The Girl Who Wanted to Hunt* were collected in Siberia by Waldemar Bogoras in the 1890s, by L.Y. Sternberg in 1904, and by Dmitri Nagishkin in 1975.

All these stories tell of challenges that must be met in order for a young woman to claim her maturing female powers. What seems unique about Anga is that she is initiated into a traditionally male domain—hunting. This might not have seemed unusual to the native peoples living in the Amur-Ussuri river region of southeastern Siberia. The Udeghes, Nanais, and others designated both men and women to conduct rituals for healing, burying the dead, and attracting game.

Unin, however, has rigid notions of "girl's work." Anga displays the extraordinary powers of a potential shaman, but the jealous, evil Unin drives her stepdaughter away. From her celestial home on the moon, Anga is said to give hope and comforting dreams to children everywhere, especially to those who are orphans like her.

—E.B.

Artist's Note: The pictures in this book were painted in gouache on Whatman cold press 140 lb. watercolor paper, with final touches added in color pencil. Borders and graphic embellishments were inspired by the highly sophisticated decorative art and ritual artifacts of the Udeghe, Nanai, and other indigenous peoples of the Amur River region. —D.B.